HELEN HALL LIBRARY
City of League City
100 West Walker
League City, TX 77573-3899

D0757600

Angelfish

by Colleen Sexton

HELEN HALL LIBRARY
100 Walker St
League City, TX 77573

DISCARD

BLASTOFF!
2
READERS

BELLWETHER MEDIA • MINNEAPOLIS, MN

Note to Librarians, Teachers, and Parents:

Blastoff! Readers are carefully developed by literacy experts and combine standards-based content with developmentally appropriate text.

Level 1 provides the most support through repetition of high-frequency words, light text, predictable sentence patterns, and strong visual support.

Level 2 offers early readers a bit more challenge through varied simple sentences, increased text load, and less repetition of high-frequency words.

Level 3 advances early-fluent readers toward fluency through increased text and concept load, less reliance on visuals, longer sentences, and more literary language.

Level 4 builds reading stamina by providing more text per page, increased use of punctuation, greater variation in sentence patterns, and increasingly challenging vocabulary.

Level 5 encourages children to move from "learning to read" to "reading to learn" by providing even more text, varied writing styles, and less familiar topics.

Whichever book is right for your reader, Blastoff! Readers are the perfect books to build confidence and encourage a love of reading that will last a lifetime!

This edition first published in 2009 by Bellwether Media, Inc.

No part of this publication may be reproduced in whole or in part without written permission of the publisher. For information regarding permission, write to Bellwether Media, Inc., Attention: Permissions Department, Post Office Box 19349, Minneapolis, MN 55419.

Library of Congress Cataloging-in-Publication Data
Sexton, Colleen A., 1967–
  Angelfish / by Colleen Sexton.
     p. cm. – (Blastoff! readers. Oceans alive)
  Includes bibliographical references and index.
  Summary: "Simple text and supportive images introduce beginning readers to angelfish. Intended for students in kindergarten through third grade"–Provided by publisher.
  ISBN-13: 978-1-60014-248-2 (hardcover : alk. paper)
  ISBN-10: 1-60014-248-6 (hardcover : alk. paper)
  1. Marine angelfishes–Juvenile literature. I. Title.

  QL638.P768S49 2009
  597'.72–dc22   2008033539

Text copyright © 2009 by Bellwether Media, Inc. BLASTOFF! READERS and associated logos are trademarks and/or registered trademarks of Bellwether Media, Inc.

SCHOLASTIC, CHILDREN'S PRESS, and associated logos are trademarks and/or registered trademarks of Scholastic Inc. Printed in the United States of America.

Contents

Angelfish are colorful fish that live in warm ocean waters.

They live in and around
coral reefs.

Most angelfish live in pairs
made up of one female
and one male.

Some angelfish live in groups. A male protects a **territory** for himself and several females.

There are more than 80 different kinds of angelfish.

Some are the size of your finger. Others are as long as your arm!

Angelfish are known for their bright colors. They can be one color or many colors.

The color of an angelfish
can change as it grows.

Angelfish can have stripes, spots, or other **patterns**.

These patterns hide them from **predators**. Angelfish blend in with the coral reef.

Angelfish have flat bodies.

Their skin is covered with rough **scales**.

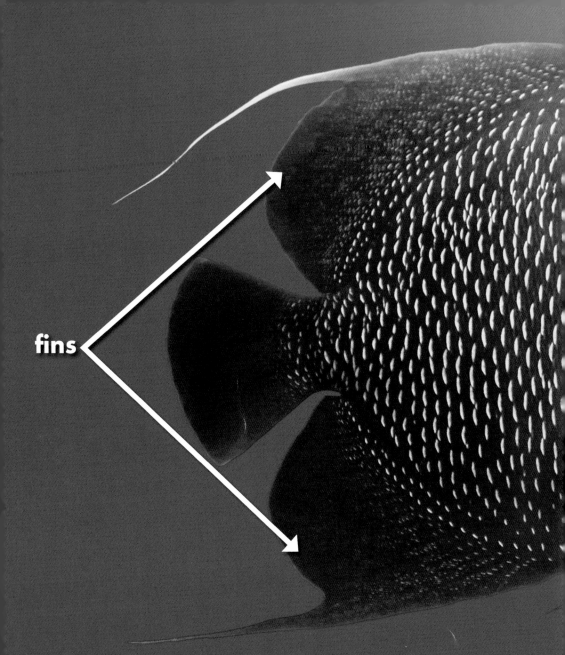

fins

Angelfish move their long **fins** and tail back and forth to swim.

gills

Angelfish breathe through **gills**.

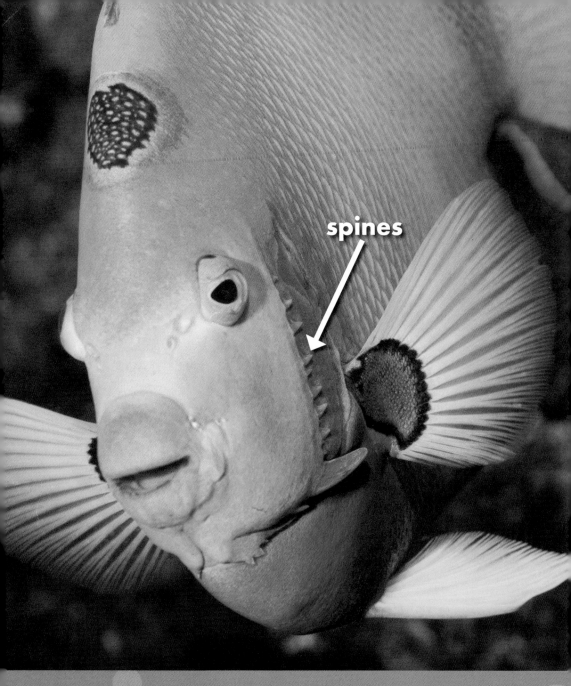

spines

Angelfish have sharp **spines** by their cheeks. The spines warn predators to stay away.

They have small mouths filled with tiny teeth. Angelfish eat corals, sponges, and **algae**.

Some angelfish eat tiny animals and plants off the bodies of larger ocean animals.

They help keep the larger
animals clean and healthy!

Glossary

algae—living things that grow in water

coral reef—a structure in the ocean made of the skeletons of many small, tube-shaped animals called corals

fins—flaps on a fish's body used for moving, steering, and stopping in the water

gills—organs near the mouth that a fish uses to breathe; the gills move oxygen from the water to the fish's blood.

pattern—an arrangement of lines and shapes

predator—an animal that hunts other animals for food

scales—small, hard plates that cover the bodies of many fish

spine—a hard, sharp part on an animal or plant

territory—an area that animals live in and defend

To Learn More

AT THE LIBRARY

Earle, Sylvia A. *Hello, Fish! Visiting the Coral Reef.* Washington, D.C.: National Geographic Society, 1999.

Landau, Elaine. *Angelfish.* New York: Children's Press, 1999.

Wu, Norbert. *Fish Faces.* New York: Holt, 1993.

ON THE WEB

Learning more about angelfish is as easy as 1, 2, 3.

1. Go to www.factsurfer.com.

2. Enter "angelfish" into the search box.

3. Click the "Surf" button and you will see a list of related Web sites.

With factsurfer.com, finding more information is just a click away.

Index

The images in this book are reproduced through the courtesy of: Jeff Hunter, front cover, pp. 14, 15, 20-21; Steffen Foerster Photography, p. 4; Georgette Douwma, pp. 5, 11, 12-13; blickwinkel / Alamy, pp. 6-7; Ian Scott, pp. 8-9, 10; Qldian, pp. 16-17; Stephen Frink, p. 18; Reinhard Dirscherl, p. 19.